SOLVING

GOD

THE

PUZZLE

CAN WE KNOW WITH
CERTAINTY GOD EXISTS?

TOM HAMMOND

Solving the God Puzzle

Published by:
GPM
3070 Windward Plaza, Ste. F301
Alpharetta, GA 30005

Edited by Lynn Copeland

Illustrations by Dennis Auth (dennisauth.com)

Design and production by Genesis Group (genesisgroup.net)

ISBN 978-1-7340532-6-5

Printed in India

Imagine you are shipwrecked alone on a deserted tropical island, running a blistering fever and coughing so violently your lungs ache. Nothing but a few pieces of luggage have washed ashore, one of which contains a bottle of pills with a note that says "These tablets will either cure all tropical diseases or kill you on the spot. I'm not sure which." You don't know what you should do, so you decide to do nothing and hope for the best.

That's what a lot people do when it comes to the question of God's existence. Believing it's like a blind man in a dark room looking for a black cat that isn't there, they conclude that finding the truth about God's existence is either impossible or so unlikely that it's not worth trying.

But is it really that hopeless? Is solving the puzzle about whether or not God exists really that difficult? I hope you stick around to find out. If it turns out we can find a solution, nothing less than your eternal destination is at stake.

AGNOSTICISM

The belief that we can't know with certainty whether God exists is the bedrock principle of a worldview called "agnosticism." *Agnostics* are different from *theists* (people who believe God exists) and *atheists* (people who believe the exact opposite) in that they try to remain neutral on the subject, being willing to admit God *might* exist, and just as willing to admit He might not. Whether it's because they believe there's not enough reliable information to make a firm decision, or because they wish to avoid offending someone who has already taken a side, agnostics choose to opt out on the question of God's existence altogether.

Interestingly, there are a couple of aspects to agnosticism that many don't realize. First, though in recent years the word "agnostic" more commonly means "not knowable," its original meaning is rooted in what the ancient Greeks called "ignorance." Simply put, an agnostic was someone short on knowledge. Second, agnosticism is a worldview based on faith rather than fact. As a matter of fact, in one sense *all* worldviews are based on faith. Let me explain.

Theism, atheism, and agnosticism are all "faith-based" in the sense they cannot be proven true or false *just* by looking at evidence. That's to say, *how people interpret evidence depends on which worldview they bring to it*. That's why theists and atheists can both look at the same fossil and come away with entirely different conclusions about it. It all depends on which worldview they have already embraced.

Because a belief is "faith-based" doesn't mean it is false, nor does it mean it is a blind faith without any evidence to support it. There can be very good reasons (and evidences) for putting one's faith in a belief, as well as very good reasons (and evidences) for why not to.

Consequently, a worldview must first be evaluated on the basis of its rationality and logic (as well as how it lines up with reality) before we can know if it *rightly* interprets evidence. Since I suspect you want to be both rational and logical (and above all, not be "ignorant"), I'm guessing you want to see if your worldview passes the test. Keep reading and we'll see how it measures up.

There are many versions of "theism," with pantheism, polytheism, and monotheism being the most common. Throughout this booklet the term "theism" will refer to monotheism—the belief that there is only one God—and specifically the belief in the existence of the Judeo-Christian God of the Bible.

AGNOSTICISM'S UNDERLYING BELIEFS

We believe many things because we first hold preceding (or underlying) beliefs that give rise to them. For instance, we might believe it's a good idea to carry an umbrella with us because we've first believed it's likely to rain. Or, we might believe we should fill up our fuel tank because we've first believed it will soon be empty. Agnosticism, like all worldviews, is arrived at the same way.

But are agnosticism's underlying beliefs really that solid? Do they make sense, and do they give us good reasons for putting our faith in agnosticism? To answer these questions, we will examine some of the more commonly held underlying beliefs of agnosticism to see if they are illogical, or perhaps even "self-defeating." Because there may be eternal consequences if agnosticism proves to be false, understanding its underlying beliefs is crucial.

> When a statement is "self-defeating," it means the statement can't possibly be true because it cancels itself out. For example, the statement "I am certain we can't know anything with certainty" is a self-defeating proposition. If we really are certain we can't know anything with certainty, then the statement is obviously false. You might say self-defeating statements commit suicide every time they are stated.

UNDERLYING BELIEF #1: We Can't Believe in God's Existence Until Science Proves It

When agnostics say there isn't enough evidence to confidently believe in a supernatural God's

7

existence, they usually mean there isn't the kind of evidence that will force people to believe in God even if they don't wish to. In a sense this is true. Scientists can't go into a laboratory and perform measurable, objective experiments on anything that is by definition "metaphysical" (something that transcends both space and time, like a supernatural God).

Conversely, atheists can't go into a laboratory and scientifically prove God *doesn't* exist for the very same reasons. Therefore, insisting on this kind of scientific proof of God's existence (or non-existence) is inconsistent with scientific realities, which makes it an irrational demand.

But there's another problem with this belief that makes it self-defeating. If we say we can't believe in anything unless science first proves it, then before the statement itself can be believed science must first prove the statement is true. Unfortunately for agnostics, there is no scientific proof the statement is true (otherwise, everyone would agree it is true,

8

which obviously they do not). In fact, most people (including agnostics) believe in all kinds of things science can't prove—like love, morality, and beauty. Consequently, we can't rely on science alone to tell us which worldview is true.

UNDERLYING BELIEF #2:

We Can't Believe in God's Existence Because We Are Limited

There is a well-known story about four blind men who attempted to describe an elephant just by touching the part of the elephant in front of them:

- The man standing by the elephant's trunk likened the animal to a snake.

- The one standing next to its leg likened the elephant to a tree trunk.

- The man standing along its side likened the creature to a large, smooth wall.

- The individual at its tail likened the elephant to a whip.

Because all four men had limited perception, none described the elephant accurately or in its entirety. Instead, they reached woefully

wrong conclusions because they believed their limited knowledge was the only knowledge that was available.

A lot of agnostics attempt to use illustrations like this to support the argument that because we have limited (finite) abilities to "know," we can never know anything about God's existence with certainty. But there are problems with this line of reasoning.

- First, not all people are limited in the same sense as these four blind men; otherwise, we couldn't know what they were getting wrong in describing the elephant.

- Second, there are often ways to obtain information we can't see for ourselves. So while admittedly no single one of us can know *everything* there is to know about a given subject, we can know enough to make certain decisions about it provided we have a reliable source of information (more on this in a bit).

- Finally, using illustrations like this to support agnosticism is self-defeating. If everyone's ability to know is limited, then so is the agnostic's, including what he knows about God's existence. Simply put, the agnostic can't have it both ways. If it's possible he can know enough to conclude God's existence is unknowable, it's also possible he can know enough to know God exists if in fact He does.

UNDERLYING BELIEF #3:

Agnosticism Is More Tolerant Than Other Worldviews

Many agnostics think not choosing a side on the matter of God's existence makes them more "tolerant" because they're not saying either side is wrong. But is this really the case?

The first thing we have to understand is that tolerance doesn't mean not taking a side on an issue. Tolerance means we make room for opinions or beliefs other than our own. While we might believe (for very good reasons) that a particular view is wrong, being tolerant means we still afford respect to the people who hold it.

Unfortunately, many have recently redefined tolerance to mean giving equal "value" to all beliefs, even when opposing beliefs contradict one another. "Your truth is your truth and my truth is my truth" is how we often hear it, and what it really amounts to is that no one can ever be considered wrong. That's obviously illogical. We can't rationally believe two opposing truth claims can be true at the same time and in the same context. For instance, we can't logically believe the person who says $2 + 2 = 4$ and the person who says $2 + 2 = 5$ are both right. To believe at least one of them is wrong isn't intolerant, it's just common sense.

The illogical nature of this underlying belief also makes it self-defeating. If we believe no one can ever be wrong, then we must also believe no one can ever be exclusively right—including the person who says agnosticism is true.

Agnosticism Is More Intelligent Than Other Worldviews

The belief that uncertainty about God's existence is a more intelligent approach is often the result of accepting the three underlying beliefs we've just examined. But as we've seen, those underlying beliefs are questionable for a number of reasons, which should make us wonder if agnosticism is a more intelligent worldview after all.

Another problem with this belief is that it's inconsistent with the certainty we want in most other areas of our lives. Imagine sitting on an airplane and hearing the flight attendant announce, "Welcome aboard Foggy Airlines! You'll be happy to know our pilot today is uncertain about how to fly this airplane." I doubt you would need much help in finding the nearest exit!

Finally, like the other underlying beliefs, this one is also self-defeating. If we equate uncertainty with intelligence, then we can't assert

we're certain that God's existence is unknowable without simultaneously associating the assertion with unintelligence. Perhaps we should see if certainty about God's existence and intelligence actually go hand-in-hand. After all, a little intelligence goes a long way when it comes to solving puzzles.

UNDERLYING BELIEF #5:

What We Believe About God's Existence Doesn't Matter

This may be agnosticism's most common, and most consequential, underlying belief of all. Obviously, if the claim that God's existence can't be known with certainty is true, we can all readily agree we have no idea if what we believe about it matters or not. On the other hand, if we find that God's existence *can* be known, then what we believe about it may matter more than everything else we believe put together.

With this in mind I hope you'll keep reading. The importance of solving this puzzle may be greater than you thought.

THE VERDICT ON AGNOSTICISM

By now we've seen that agnosticism's underlying beliefs aren't as rational or as logical as many believe. When we add the fact that agnosticism is built on many self-defeating assumptions, we're suddenly forced to look elsewhere for the solution to God's existence.

But can either Christian theism or atheism pass the tests of rationality and logic? More importantly, can either be worthy of our faith? I believe if we look at just Christian theism's underlying beliefs we can answer this question rather quickly. That's not to ignore atheism. It's just that atheism's underlying beliefs are usually the exact (or very near) opposite of Christianity's, so if Christian theism's underlying beliefs are rational and logical, it's safe to assume atheism's aren't. Let me show you why.

A CLOSER LOOK AT CHRISTIAN THEISM

Just like agnostics, Christian theists hold many underlying beliefs that point them to their worldview. Let's look at some of those beliefs and see how well they match up with reality. While we're at it, let's make certain they aren't illogical or self-defeating. If it turns out they are, Christian theism will fare no better than agnosticism as the solution to our puzzle.

UNDERLYING BELIEF #1: **The Universe Had a Beginning**

As previously mentioned, the worldview we bring to scientific evidence determines how we interpret it, but Christian theism's belief that the universe had a beginning actually finds strong objective support in a scientific axiom called the Second Law of Thermodynamics.

Without diving into its complexities, this scientific reality tells us that over time isolated systems—like our universe—tend to become less organized (more chaotic) and have less available energy (like heat) doing any "work." This means if the universe has always existed, it would have already degenerated into an unorganized, chaotic heap long before now, with too little useful energy left to sustain life. Because this obviously isn't the case, *we know our universe had a beginning—and a relatively recent one.*

Granted, not all atheists disagree that our universe had a beginning, but for an atheist any "beginning" had to be self-instigated. And as we are about to see, that notion opens up a whole new can of worms...

Though some believe our universe may be just one of multiple universes, or that it may have been spawned from a parent universe or a series of universes, throughout this booklet the term "universe" will refer to the totality of all space, matter, and energy since the beginning of time.

UNDERLYING
BELIEF #2:

The Universe Had a Creator

Because our universe had a beginning, something other than itself must have triggered it. Guns don't shoot all by themselves, and things like universes don't just pop into existence out of absolutely nothing. That is, unless something causes them to.

Christian theists believe an eternal, uncreated creator must exist for anything else to exist. (Aristotle, the famous Greek philosopher who lived centuries ago, called this uncreated creator "The Unmoved Mover.") So why must the creator be both uncreated and eternal? Because there has to be a first "uncaused" instigator (or cause) that causes everything else. Otherwise, we are forced to believe everything came from absolutely nothing: no space, no time, no energy, no anything. Not only that, we are also forced to believe that even if such a thing were possible (which it is not), it all brought itself into existence for no reason whatsoever.

Obviously, to believe everything came from absolutely nothing is absurd. There simply has to be an eternally existing first cause (creator) from which time and events began rolling forward. Not only do Christian theists believe this eternally existing first cause must exist, they also believe it is appropriately called "God."

The Creator Must Be All-Powerful

The sheer magnitude of the energy we see in our universe tells us the creator must possess unimaginable power. Consider our sun. It's just one relatively small star out of hundreds of billions of stars that comprise our galaxy (which is just one galaxy out of many billions that comprise our universe), yet this average-sized blazing ball of hot gas is generating energy from 450 million tons of matter every time your heart beats. If you're not a physicist that might not impress you much, but compared to the totality of the power that drives our universe, our sun doesn't amount to a drop in the ocean.

Christian theists believe all this power could not exist without an incredibly powerful source to both account for and organize it. Simply put, they believe all this power requires a creator that possesses enough power to cause and control it.

The Creator Must Be Supernatural

Christian theists believe the uncreated creator must exist *outside* our natural universe, transcending both time and space. The reason is simple: if the creator existed as part of our universe (in such a way that its existence *depended* on our universe), then it couldn't have existed *before* the universe was created in order to create it.

There are only two ways out of this conundrum. We can say the creator existed before He created Himself so He could then create Himself (a ridiculous conclusion), or we can simply acknowledge that He is self-sufficient, supernatural, and exists outside the dimensions of our universe.

Oh, wait. Did I just say "He"?

The Creator Must Be a Personal Being

Christian theists believe the creator thinks with a mind, and has the ability to initiate determined actions stemming from the thoughts of

His mind. In other words, Christian theists believe the creator is not a random, mindless "force" (like electrical energy), but rather is a conscious, personal being who decides to do things with intentional purposes.

When you consider the mathematical implications of incredible complexities like DNA coming into existence solely from the random workings of chance, it's easy to see why. The evidence indicates our universe is much more the product of an intentional idea than the result of an unintentional cosmic accident.

Go to SolvingtheGodPuzzle.com to see the mathematical nightmare of trying to believe a living, functioning cell could come into existence solely by virtue of the unthinking laws of nature.

IS CHRISTIAN THEISM VIABLE?

We've just seen that Christian theism's beliefs about reality aren't self-defeating. They can all be stated without proving themselves false just by doing so. Neither are they irrational. They all make logical sense, and there is no objective interpretation of any scientific evidence that proves them false (just some highly subjective interpretations that try to).

The implications are clear: unlike agnosticism, Christian theism doesn't eliminate itself as a credible worldview by being self-defeating and illogical, and unlike atheism, it doesn't ask us to believe in impossibilities (like the universe existing eternally, or that it caused itself). This means Christian theism's beliefs about reality and its need for a creator are consistent with what we can see and are in accord with what we can know.

But this raises another question: Can we know it is Christian theism's God who exists (as we've been assuming), or must we stop at just recognizing that a creator of some kind must be out there? I propose we can *know* Christian theism's God exists—if we can know our source of information is reliable. That's a huge piece of our puzzle, and one we need to seriously consider.

WE CAN KNOW THE GOD OF THE BIBLE EXISTS

Let's take a moment and consider something. As we've just read, there are solid reasons to believe reality demands the following:

- The universe had a beginning.

- This beginning was caused by an eternal, uncreated creator appropriately called "God."

- "God" is unimaginably powerful.

- "God" is supernatural.

- "God" is a person who thinks.

Now let's compare all this to what the Bible says:

- The universe had a beginning.[1]

- God is its eternally existing creator.[2]

- God is unimaginably powerful.[3]

- God is supernatural.[4]

- God is a person who thinks.[5]

Regardless of what you believed about God or the Bible before coming to this booklet, it's difficult to deny that the God reality demands and the God the Bible describes are one and the same. Of course, this doesn't prove anything else the Bible says about God is true. We'll have to look just a bit further to see what we can know on that issue. Fortunately, there's a shortcut.

WE CAN KNOW THE BIBLE IS A RELIABLE SOURCE OF INFORMATION

If you're an agnostic, you're not sold on the trustworthiness of the Bible; otherwise, you wouldn't still be an agnostic. But what I'm about to show you should change your mind. While this small book can't begin to cover all the scholarship that confirms the Bible's accuracy and authenticity, nor address all the accusations that have been hurled against it, we can look at one relatively small section of the Bible and determine whether we can trust everything else it says.

Specifically, I want us to consider the first four books in the New Testament (Matthew,

Mark, Luke, and John), which are commonly called "the Gospels" ("gospel" is Greek for "good news"). It's here we read what Christianity claims are the eyewitness accounts of the life and ministry of Jesus of Nazareth, a man these eyewitnesses say was born some two thousand years ago in the land of Israel, performed many miracles, was executed on a Roman cross, and then was resurrected from the dead.

But what is undoubtedly these eyewitnesses' most astonishing claim is that Jesus was God Himself![6] Obviously, that's a monumental declaration. And because everything else Christianity teaches about God depends on this claim being true, the importance of determining the trustworthiness of these eyewitnesses cannot be overstated.

So, are there any corroborating facts we can consider that establish the eyewitnesses' credibility? Are there good reasons to believe Christian theism's trust in these writers is warranted? I believe there are many very good reasons, but we'll look at just three.

REASON #1: **The Gospels Were Written Too Early to Be Myths**

The first three Gospels—Matthew, Mark, and Luke—were all written by the early AD 60s (John was written some twenty to thirty years later). That means three of the four Gospels were written within thirty years of Jesus' lifetime. This is important because it usually takes two or three generations before a legend or myth can take root. As long as people are still alive who can credibly refute a lie, it's unlikely the lie will gain widespread belief. There is no doubt Christianity gained widespread acceptance within just a few short years of the life, death, and resurrection of Jesus. Apparently, there weren't any credible naysayers.

REASON #2: **The Gospels Are Too Embarrassing to Be Myths**

If people wanted to write bogus eyewitness accounts of the life of Jesus in order to fashion themselves as beloved leaders of a new false religion, they wouldn't include their own failings and shortcomings while doing so. The Gospels contain several details about the eyewitnesses that are embarrassing to say the least (read them and you'll see for yourself what I mean). The only plausible reason for this is that the eyewitnesses believed telling the truth mattered more than defending their reputations.

REASON #3: **The Gospels Were Too Costly to Be Myths**

People won't willingly die for what they know is a lie. Every Gospel writer risked death for his testimony. If they had known their testimonies were false, they each would have said, "Hold on, everyone, I just made all this stuff up!" Not a single one did. Why? Because they *knew* Jesus was God and that everything they said about Him was true. There was simply no denying it!

OK, you may be thinking, *but what about the rest of the Bible? Can we trust everything else it has to say?* Based on the fact that we have three solid reasons to believe the Gospels are trustworthy, I believe we can have equal confidence that the rest of the Bible is trustworthy too.

Here's why:

- If the Gospels are reliable, we have every reason to believe Jesus was, and is, God. In His teachings Jesus often referred to the Old Testament, which was written well before His lifetime on earth, and He never once said that anything in it was untrue or needed correction. Considering the Old Testament is a major component of the Bible (which is God's divine revelation to man), if anything in it was false, we can safely assume Jesus would have addressed it.

- The remainder of the New Testament was written by the same people who wrote the four Gospels, or by people they intimately knew. If everything these writers said in the Gospels is so true it was worth dying for if need be, there is no plausible reason to suspect the rest of the New Testament isn't true as well.

In a nutshell, because we can know the Gospels are true, we can know both the Old Testament and the remainder of the New Testament are also true.

WHY AREN'T AGNOSTICS AND ATHEISTS CONVINCED GOD EXISTS?

As we've seen, agnosticism claims there aren't sufficient reasons to confidently believe God exists, while atheism claims there are good reasons to believe He doesn't. But because we've also seen that neither of these worldviews measure up with reality, it should make us wonder, *Why are there still agnostics and atheists?*

The Bible says it's because agnostics and atheists "suppress the truth" about God and His existence. Why? Because they want to live as they please rather than submit their lives to Him, even when God has made His existence so obvious they have no excuse for denying it:

> But God shows his anger from heaven against all sinful, wicked people who suppress the truth by their wickedness. They know the truth about God because he has made it obvious to them. For ever since the world was created, people have seen the earth and sky. Through everything God made, they can clearly see his invisible qualities—his eternal power and divine

nature. So they have no excuse for not knowing God. (Romans 1:18–20, NLT)

This passage tells us that people's rejection of God isn't based on sound reasoning; rather, they reject Him simply because they choose to. It also tells us every person really knows God exists. But the most frightening thing it tells us is that there will be horrific consequences for choosing to suppress this undeniable truth. So horrific that there are some facts we need to understand.

FACT #1:   **Absolute Morality Exists**

Many people think morality is relative rather than absolute. That's to say, they believe what's right for one person may not be right for everyone, or what's considered moral in one society isn't necessarily moral for all societies. The Bible says this isn't true, that absolute morality exists and that even our consciences know it.[7] If you doubt it, consider the following.

If it's true there is no such thing as absolute morality, then it's possible that at certain times or in certain situations sexually abusing children is perfectly fine. But does any healthy minded person really believe this? Of course not. Every sane person agrees that sexually abusing a child is just plain wrong! Always. No exceptions. And child sexual abuse isn't the only example we could use. What about racism? Is racism ever "morally acceptable"? Or rape? Can you think of a circumstance where rape should be overlooked because it's morally OK? Again, the answer is always no!

This means there are moral values that are absolute. We just intuitively know they apply at all times to all people under all circumstances. The reason we all instinctively know there are absolute morals is that every one of us has been made in the image of God and has His moral Law written on our hearts.[8]

FACT #2:

Morality Originates in a Perfectly Moral God

Because we know there are certain moral values that are absolute, the next question is, where do these moral values originate? Are they arbitrary, reflecting nothing more than opinions or preferences? Or do they come from something far deeper and more concrete?

Some people believe morality is a byproduct of evolution. They speculate that the early humans who adopted certain moral beliefs had better chances of survival, and these moral beliefs were passed down (in some unknown way or other) to subsequent generations. But when you think about it, this hypothesis doesn't hold up.

The theory of evolution depends on "survival of the fittest," and any trait that looks out for the benefit of anyone beyond the individual (or the individual's immediate family or clan) is contrary to evolution's supposed mechanism. Furthermore, it's hard to make the case that an individual caring about a child being sexually abused in some far off region had any effect on the individual's own chances of survival.

So, if morality isn't a product of evolution, where did these moral absolutes come from? We simply have to look no further than God. The One who created us gave us each a conscience, instilling in us the knowledge of right and wrong. It is He, and He alone, who determines morality. What gives Him this right? Well, besides the fact He is God, He is also morally perfect in His every thought, word, and deed.[9] This means morality is not something God arbitrarily declares, it is a reflection of who He is.

Unfortunately, morality is also a reflection of us.

FACT #3: **All People (Including You and Me) Are Sinners**

The Bible says everyone—including you—is a sinner.[10] *Wait a minute*, you may be thinking, *I haven't raped anyone, I'm not a racist, and I certainly haven't sexually abused a child!* I would hope you haven't. But the Bible says if you've broken just one of God's moral laws (the Ten Commandments)—like telling a lie, taking something that wasn't yours, disobeying your parents, using God's name in vain, or having sexually immoral thoughts—you're just as guilty as if you'd broken them all.[11] And you may as well admit you've broken at least one of them. We all have. But why?

"Sin" is any thought, word, or action that violates or rebels against God's moral law or will. You might say it's any kind of disobedience to God or deviation from acting or thinking in accordance with His character.

The Bible says we sin because we are born with a sin nature.[12] You don't believe it? When was the last time you saw a small child who had to be taught to be selfish, mean, or dishonest? You know these sinful behaviors come just as naturally to a small child as do eating and sleeping.[13] What's more, this innate desire to sin and rebel against God's moral laws remains with us through-out our life-times.[14]

OK, you might think, *if sinning is just part of who I am, what's the big deal?* Well, the big deal is this: though we are born with a desire to sin, God gave us a conscience so we'd know right from wrong, and He holds us accountable for our sinful choices. God hates sin and will punish all guilty sinners. When you see the details, it's downright terrifying.

FACT #4:

All Sinners (Including You and Me) Are Condemned to Hell

The idea of Hell as our eternal destination for our sin is something a lot of people struggle with. They can't understand how a good God could condemn anyone to a place of eternal torment, especially for sins that don't seem very significant to us. ("OK, so what if I told a little lie? It's not like I killed somebody!") That's because they don't understand the true nature or character of God.

God alone is perfectly righteous.[15] One who is perfectly righteous can't condone a moral imperfection of any kind, regardless of how small we might think it is. That's why God can't overlook even the smallest of sins and pretend it didn't happen. If He did, He'd be less than perfect.

Consequently, perfect righteousness de-mands perfect judgment, and because God is a perfectly righteous judge,[16] He has determined the sentence on all moral lawbreakers is death and condemnation to an eternal prison called Hell.[17,18] Why is the sentence so harsh? Because it reflects just how holy and perfect God's char-acter and standards really are. But before you panic, there's another side to God's character you absolutely need to know. In fact, it's the most amazing thing you'll ever hear.

I've been waiting this entire book to tell you about it!

FACT #5:

God Loves Sinners, and Can Save Them from Death and Hell

You might want to read this fact again. What it means is simply this: regardless of how many moral laws you've broken, or how many times you've broken them, God can forgive you, grant you everlasting life, and save you from Hell. Whether you've had an abortion, been convicted of a heinous crime, or done something you may think is even worse, God can grant you a full pardon for every sin you've ever committed!

But how can He do this? How can a perfectly righteous God who can't possibly overlook your sins save you from the sentence you so richly deserve? The answer is in Jesus Christ, the Son of God. More specifically, it's in Jesus' sacrificial death on the cross that He suffered *on your behalf*, making it possible for God to forgive you and let you live eternally with Him in Heaven. Yes, you read that correctly. Jesus was willing to die in your place so you can go free![19]

Though Jesus died on the cross, He didn't remain in the grave. Three days later He rose from the dead, victorious over death, thus proving He is indeed the living Son of God!

Why would Jesus suffer the death penalty for sinners, you ask? Well, as incredible as it sounds, God still loves sinners and wants to lavish His infinite kindness and mercy on them, giving them eternal life.[20,21] To receive this amazing free gift, here is what the Bible calls you to do:

- Confess to God that you're a guilty sinner who has failed to perfectly keep His moral laws

- Acknowledge Jesus is the resurrected Lord, and repent of (turn away from) your sins

- Put your trust (faith) in Jesus Christ, believing His death paid the penalty in full for sinners

That's the sum of it! Trying to be a good person won't save you, going to church won't save you, being baptized won't save you, nor will any other religious activity or ritual. You can be saved only by grace (God's undeserved favor) through faith in Jesus alone.[22,23]

When you do that, here's what happens:

- You will have new priorities and desires because you have been given a new heart.[24]

- You will be declared holy, blameless, and beyond reproach.[25]

- You will no longer stand condemned before God.[26]

Instead, you will be adopted as a child of God,[27] making you an heir to all the blessings of Heaven.[28] It's just a matter of deciding where to put your faith:

- in a worldview like agnosticism or atheism that offers nothing,

or

- in the Lord Jesus Christ who offers you forgiveness and eternal life.

THE MOST IMPORTANT DECISION OF YOUR LIFE

If agnosticism had proved true, it would mean Jesus was a liar. He not only claimed to be the truth,[29] He said you could *know* the truth (meaning Himself) and that *knowing* the truth would set you free.[30] But set free from what?

For one thing, you can be set free from the anxiety of wondering what will happen when you die. For another, you can be set free from the sentence of death and Hell you now stand to receive. But most astonishing of all, you can be set free from all your doubts about God's existence because you will *know Him* and be in a personal relationship with Him.

But be sure of this: these freedoms won't become a reality until you repent of your sins and put your faith in Jesus Christ, believing He is the living Son of God, who through His death paid the penalty for sinners, and through His resurrection proved He is all He claims to be. There is simply no other way.

So what will it be? Are you ready to climb down off agnosticism's fence and experience life like you've never known it before, filled with the purpose, meaning, and hope God wants for you? Or will you choose to stay where you are, needlessly clinging to the doubts that lead to death and certain damnation?

The idea of God and His existence doesn't have to be a puzzle. Not when Jesus is our solution.

FIRST STEPS

If you have just responded to Jesus Christ in repentance and faith, having surrendered your life to His control, congratulations, and welcome to the family of God! Of course, you are also probably wondering, *OK, now what?* Here is a short list of things you should immediately begin focusing on. Keep in mind this is very basic information. For additional resources offering a fuller, deeper discussion on these and many other topics, please go to Solvingthe GodPuzzle.com.

1. **Start reading the Bible.** The Bible is God's revelation of Himself to mankind, so you will want to begin reading it daily to learn more about this amazing God who saved you. After all, He created you to know Him. God's Word, the Bible, is also our authoritative source for instructions on how we should live, think, worship, and serve. While there are many good translations of the Bible available, we recommend the New American Standard Bible, the New King James Version, or the New Living Translation (go to SolvingtheGodPuzzle.com and click on "Choosing a Bible" to learn more about their differences).

   We suggest you begin with the Gospel of John in the New Testament. If you run into passages you don't understand, don't become discouraged. Just keep reading, and start applying the passages you do understand. Before long, as you become more familiar with other portions of the Bible, a lot of the difficult passages will become clearer, and you will become more confident in your understanding.

2. **Start praying to God on a consistent basis.** God communicates to us through the Bible, and we communicate with Him through prayer. The Bible tells us to pray continually (1 Thessalonians 5:17). Our prayers should include thanksgiving (Philippians 4:6), praise (Hebrews 13:15), confession (1 John 1:9), and petitions for ourselves and for others (1 Peter 5:6,7; Ephesians 6:18). Always remember, if we truly want to know God, we must talk with Him daily and seek His guidance in our lives.

3. **Find a church family.** I said earlier that going to church won't save you, but the Bible teaches us not to give up meeting together (Hebrews 10:25). To live as Christ wants us to, we need the love, encouragement, and strength we get from fellow believers. We are also commanded to offer

back those same blessings in return. The most effective way we can do this is through personal relationships with our fellow believers. The church is a community of believers where these relationships can be established and nurtured. To help you decide which church is right for you, see "Choosing a Church" at SolvingtheGod Puzzle.com.

4. **Be baptized as a new believer.** Again, it is very important to understand that the act of baptism does not save us. If we have repented of our sins and put our faith in Jesus Christ, we are already saved. But being baptized is a critical act of obedience to the Lord, and serves as an outward testimony of what God has now done in our lives. In fact, Jesus tells us that if we are ashamed of Him and His words, He will be ashamed of us when He comes in His glory (Luke 9:26). While various methods of baptism are offered, we believe "immersion" best reflects the New Testament model of baptism (Acts 8:38), and best demonstrates that God has now resurrected us to a new, spiritual life in Him (Romans 6:4).

NOTES

1. "In the beginning God created the heavens and the earth." (Genesis 1:1)

2. "Before the mountains were born or You gave birth to the earth and the world, even from everlasting to everlasting, You are God." (Psalm 90:2)

3. "Oh, Lord GOD! Behold, You have made the heavens and the earth by Your great power and by Your outstretched arm! Nothing is too difficult for You." (Jeremiah 32:17)

4. "But will God indeed dwell on the earth? Behold, heaven and the highest heaven cannot contain You." (1 Kings 8:27)

5. "How precious also are Your thoughts for me, God! How vast is the sum of them!" (Psalm 139:17)

6. "He said to them, 'But who do you yourselves say that I am?' Simon Peter answered, 'You are the Christ, the Son of the living God.'" (Matthew 16:15,16)

7. "…they show the work of the Law written in their hearts, their conscience testifying and their thoughts alternately accusing or else defending them." (Romans 2:15)

8. "Then God said, 'Let Us make mankind in Our image, according to Our likeness…'" (Genesis 1:26)

9. "Therefore you shall be perfect, as your heavenly Father is perfect." (Matthew 5:48)

10. "For all have sinned and fall short of the glory of God." (Romans 3:23)

11. "For whoever keeps the whole Law, yet stumbles in one point, has become guilty of all." (James 2:10)

12. "Indeed, there is not a righteous person on earth who always does good and does not ever sin." (Ecclesiastes 7:20)

13. "...for the intent of man's heart is evil from his youth." (Genesis 8:21)

14. "Then the LORD saw that the wickedness of mankind was great on the earth, and that every intent of the thoughts of their hearts was only evil continually." (Genesis 6:5)

15. "His work is perfect, for all His ways are just; a God of faithfulness and without injustice, righteous and just is He." (Deuteronomy 32:4)

16. "You are righteous, LORD, and Your judgments are right." (Psalm 119:137)

17. "For the wages of sin is death." (Romans 6:23)

18. "You snakes, you offspring of vipers, how will you escape the sentence of hell?" (Matthew 23:33)

19. "But God demonstrates His own love toward us, in that while we were still sinners, Christ died for us." (Romans 5:8)

20. "But God, being rich in mercy, because of His great love with which He loved us, even when we were dead in our wrongdoings, made us alive together with Christ (by grace you have been saved)." (Ephesians 2:4,5)

21. "Jesus said to her, 'I am the resurrection and the life; the one who believes in Me will live, even if he dies, and everyone who lives and believes in Me will never die.'" (John 11:25,26)

22. "But when the kindness of God our Savior and His love for mankind appeared, He saved us, not on the basis of deeds which we did in righteousness, but in accordance with His mercy." (Titus 3:4,5)

23. "For by grace you have been saved through faith; and this is not of yourselves, it is the gift of God; not a result of works, so that no one may boast." (Ephesians 2:8,9)

24. "I will give you a new heart and put a new spirit within you; and I will remove the heart of stone from your flesh and give you a heart of flesh." (Ezekiel 36:26)

25. "And although you were previously alienated and hostile in attitude, engaged in evil deeds, yet He has now reconciled you in His body of flesh through death, in order to present you before Him holy and blameless and beyond reproach." (Colossians 1:21,22)

26. "Therefore there is now no condemnation at all for those who are in Christ Jesus." (Romans 8:1)

27. "But as many as received Him, to them He gave the right to become children of God, to those who believe in His name." (John 1:12)

28. "Blessed be the God and Father of our Lord Jesus Christ, who according to His great mercy has caused us to be born again to a living hope through the resurrection of Jesus Christ from the dead, to obtain an inheritance which is imperishable, undefiled, and will not fade away, reserved in heaven for you." (1 Peter 1:3,4)

29. "Jesus said to him, 'I am the way, and the truth, and the life; no one comes to the Father except through Me.'" (John 14:6)

30. "If you continue in My word, then you are truly My disciples; and you will know the truth, and the truth will set you free." (John 8:31,32)